Elsie
Saves The Day!

A Story About Using Your Talent for Good

Laura Joy Pewitt
Illustrated by Jack Whitney

Elsie Saves the Day!
Copyright © 2022 by Laura Joy Pewitt

Published by
Laura Joy Pewitt
website: laurajoypewitt.com
laurajoypewitt@gmail.com

ISBN
978-0-578-38733-8 (paperback)
978-0-578-39036-9 (ebook)

Illustrated by Jack Whitney
Designed by Darlene Swanson • van-garde.com

Printed in the USA

To - Chander - from Aunt Wezey !

"Your talent can be
your superpower.

Use it for good."

LJP

Laura Joy Pewitt
2022

Matthew 5:16

Once there was a nest of eggs high in a tall tree.
It was the perfect home for a family of birds.

Today, the eggs began to hatch.

Soon, mama bird had four babies who were hungry
and ready to eat.

Each day, mama brought them food and the little birds grew quickly. They ate worms and passed the time with chirps and laughter in their nest. Most of the birds looked forward to the day of their first flying lesson.

"I'm going to be a great flier," said Bo, "just wait and see!" Mama bird didn't care for bragging and boasting. She told the group, "I'll teach you all to be good fliers."

"Bo," she continued, "you must not brag …you should practice your singing like the others." They're all becoming very good at singing, but you could use a little more practice."

Bo thought that singing was for the birds ... the other birds, not him. Flying was all he could think about, and he imagined that he would be the best flier of all.

The day of the birds' first flying lesson
arrived. Their wings had grown long and
sturdy, and their feathers were nice and full.
"It's a good thing you ate all those worms,"
Mama said, "now, you're ready to fly!"

Bo's sister, Elsie, sang with delight as she
ate her supper. Bo thought to himself,
"She's really becoming a good singer, but
she told me that she's afraid to fly."

Mama told them, "Watch me closely and you'll be flying in no time." She spread her wings and gave a little jump to take off. She flew gently to the grass below. "Now, come on," she said to the group, "each of you give it a try."

Although Elsie was anxious, she lined up with the other birds to take her turn at flying. Bo offered to be in the back of the line.

He wanted to be the last to fly, so all the others could watch him. He was going to dazzle them with his great talent. He wanted to show-off!

Three birds took off easily and flew gently down to the grass. Mama was very proud!

"Now, Bo it's your turn," she said, "take off and fly!"

Bo stepped up to the edge of the nest and looked down. He took a giant leap and flapped his wings. He was flying!

Bo didn't land right away. Much to the surprise of the other birds, he began to show-off. He flew fast, swooping down around the mailbox.

He **zoomed** around a birdbath and
startled another bird! **Whoosh**, he
flew like the wind! "**Yippee**," he
yelled, "**I'm flying**!" He went flying
this way and that way until finally,
he returned to the nest.

All the other birds were amazed. "Wow, Bo,"
Elsie said. "You really are a great flier, but
weren't you a little afraid?" Bo boasted,
"There's nothing to it; I knew I'd be good at it."

Day after day, he flew all around. He loved to
show off. The other birds were very impressed
and listened to his boasting, (although, it wasn't
long before his bragging began to annoy them.)

One day, Bo decided to fly a little farther from home. He soon found himself over a very large building. He noticed that as people walked up to the door, it would open. Bo was curious and wondered what was inside.

Without thinking, he flew in through the open door, just as a little girl and her father were entering the store.

"Look Daddy,' said the girl, "a bird flew in here with us!" They watched as Bo went flying through the store. The man thought to himself, "I hope that bird will find his way out of here."

Bo flew up and down, and all around. That bird thought this was the most interesting adventure he had ever had. Looking down below, he watched as the little girl and her dad picked up a cookie at the bakery. Bo was getting hungry, so he quickly swooped down and picked up a piece of cookie too!

As he ate, he wondered what the other birds were doing "Probably eating more worms," he thought to himself.

Back home, mama bird was beginning to worry about Bo. He often flew around longer than any of her other birds, but this time, he had been gone most of the day. Elsie was the most worried of all, and wondered, "What if Bo can't find his way home?" "What if he's trapped or lost?" She gathered her courage, took off flying, and went out to find him.

Soon, Elsie was over the building with the automatic doors. She flew down low and overheard the little girl and her dad as they were walking out to their car. "Daddy," the girl said, "I hope the little bird will find his way out of the store." When Elsie heard this, she knew right away that Bo must be inside!

She would need to fly in there and find him, but what if she got lost too? She planned her next moves.

Bo had been flying around the store looking for his way out, only to become confused and exhausted. Twice, he had flown into a window by mistake.

He became too tired to keep flying, so he landed on a window ledge at the back of the store. He began to worry that he might not find his way out of this place.
Bo realized he needed help.

Just then, he heard a familiar voice! Far away in the
distance, Bo heard Elsie singing. Her voice was loud
and clear! Elsie had planned to fly into the building
and perch just inside the door. "If Bo can hear me
singing," she thought, "my voice can guide him back
to this exit."

Elsie's plan was a good one! Bo followed her voice all the way to the exit. He was so happy to see her! He suddenly realized that Elsie had never bragged about being such a good singer, but she sure was!

Bo smiled at Elsie and said, "Thank you
for coming to find me; it was you and
your talent that saved the day!"

Elsie took off and led Bo back to the
nest, singing happily all the way home.

The End

About the Author

Laura Joy Pewitt, MS.Ed., is a writer and an educator. For over 30 years, she's been teaching young children. She is a wife, mom, and now, "Lolli," to her grandchildren. As a teacher, she often said that the best thing one can do to help a young child learn is to read and discuss good books together, (and don't forget to take walks and play outdoors.) She believes the brain grows by what it feeds on, so feed and nurture it well! Her creative ideas for stories come when she's outdoors, hiking in the woods, walking along the beach, or while sitting on her front porch swing in Tennessee. Her first book, "Wally, the Wayward Sea Turtle," was originally published in 2017. A favorite quote of hers comes from an unknown author who said, "Don't shine so that others can see YOU, shine so that through you, others can see HIM." To learn more, visit her website: laurajoypewitt.com

I dedicate this book to my grandchildren, Severin, Elsie, and Tucker. LJP Matthew 5:16 says…" let your light shine before others, so that they may see your good works and give glory to your Father who is in heaven."

About the Illustrator

Jack Whitney is an illustrator, living in St. Louis, Missouri. Jack grew up in middle Tennessee, where at age 4 he announced that he would become an artist, (but only after he discovered that his first two choices of becoming a tractor or a bear weren't options!) He settled on becoming an artist and has remained one his whole life.

For over 30 years, Jack has used both traditional and digital tools to create art for advertising and publishing. Lately, Jack's been revisiting his skills as a fine artist with oils, acrylics, pastels, charcoal and graphite. His portraits, like himself, can be serious or humorous.

You can learn more about Jack and his art by visiting his website: Jackwhitneyfineart.com

CPSIA information can be obtained
at www.ICGtesting.com
Printed in the USA
LVHW020447050522
717774LV00006B/31